Richard Winter was for many years professor of education at Anglia Ruskin University, Cambridge, UK. His research was mainly concerned with helping nurses, social workers and teachers to develop more reflective and creative methods of working with each other and with their patients/clients/students. For more than twenty years, he has studied and practised Buddhism and meditation at the Cambridge Buddhist Centre, and he currently teaches meditation at the Buddhist Centre for students of the Cambridge University of the Third Age.

To Jo and Jess

Richard Winter

DON'T EXPECT A STANDING OVATION

And Fifty-Eight Other Pieces of Helpful Advice

AUSTIN MACAULEY PUBLISHERS™

LONDON • CAMBRIDGE • NEW YORK • SHARJAH

A CIP catalogue record for this title is available from the British Library.

ISBN 9781398401006 (Paperback)
ISBN 9781398401013 (ePub e-book)

www.austinmacauley.com

First Published (2020)
Austin Macauley Publishers Ltd
25 Canada Square
Canary Wharf
London
E14 5LQ

A big thank you to all the people who, during the writing, offered support and helpful critical suggestions: family, friends, fellow students and teachers at the Cambridge Triratna Buddhist Community, and students who attended the 'University of the Third Age' meditation courses at the Cambridge Buddhist Centre.

Table of Contents

Preface

This book is a re-working in contemporary terms of the classical Tibetan teachings on meditation practice called 'Seven Points of Mind Training', which are traditionally presented in the form of fifty-nine separate 'lines' or 'slogans'. (The term 'slogan' is discussed on page 25)

In preparing the following interpretation of the slogans, I consulted and compared a variety of published versions (listed on page 33). One of the things they have in common is that although they are written in an engaging manner, they all assume that the reader is to some extent committed to (or at least familiar with) one or other of the Tibetan Buddhist traditions.

My purpose, in contrast, was to create a version of the slogans in which the style, vocabulary and cultural references would feel natural to readers of any 'faith' or none; anyone who is open to some sort of meditation practice as a possibly helpful response to a sense of unease – about feelings, relationships, the state of the world, or a sense of purpose in one's life, etc. I did not want references to an esoteric or otherwise strange culture to interfere with what I personally experience as the immediate appeal of the teachings, their practical, down-to-earth wisdom. Thus, I have tried to imagine readers who either have no prior knowledge of Buddhism or readers who perhaps have a slight acquaintance with Buddhism but who do not necessarily wish to commit themselves to any particular tradition.

So, whatever your faith or beliefs or hopes or anxieties, I hope you will read on and that you will feel that your concerns are addressed.

Part One:
Introduction

Prologue

Don't expect a standing ovation. When I first encountered this piece of advice, many years ago, in the context of a Buddhist study group, I laughed. And if I tell anyone else about it, they laugh too. I wonder why...Perhaps we are surprised by the contradiction in our response. On the one hand, the 'advice' is so down-to-earth and obvious that our first reaction is: 'surely I don't need to be told this'. But then we realise that, actually, we do indeed have a deep desire to be appreciated that we are hardly aware of until the moment when we notice that someone or other hasn't been as grateful as we had hoped they would be, or as grateful as we 'deserved', or as grateful as we think they 'ought' to have been! So we laugh because we are surprised that a suggestion so obvious and so clearly helpful should actually *be* surprising.

We might also be surprised that this piece of advice, which feels so much like a very contemporary joke about the sly, deceptive egotism of what goes on in our minds, was formulated over a thousand years ago, as part of a Tibetan system of Buddhist teaching and surprised also that the whole system is presented as fifty-nine 'slogans', of which 'Don't expect a Standing Ovation' is number fifty-nine.

Who Needs Fifty-Nine Pieces of Helpful Advice?

Maybe not fifty-nine and certainly not all at once, but something at least seems called for. In my own case, looking back, the cheerful optimism and energy of youth carried me along quite confidently for a time. But then, slowly, as the years went by, the questions began to mount up, and the questions never seemed to have any clear answers. What were my duties, responsibilities and values, as a husband, for example, or a parent, or a friend, or a work colleague, or as a male in a chauvinist society contested by feminism, or simply as a citizen? I kept hoping to find some solid ground for objectivity or certainty, but found I was continually left with only a worrying series of questions. There seemed to be so many conflicting points of view – some claiming certainty based on 'objective scientific evidence', some arguing that all opinions were equally valid because they all depended on one's personal perspective or culture or who is interpreting the evidence. How then could I feel confidence in my decisions? What it boiled down to was: what is the right thing to do; how should I lead my life?

And these questions led on to even more general questions. How do I know things? How do I know that I *understand* something? Is my *experience* 'objective'? And, wider still: how should I relate to other people? At first, my sense that there were significant links between these questions was just a hunch. But then, quite by chance, I encountered Buddhism. Out of the blue came a request from a colleague in Thailand, engaged in a similar field of work, to work on a project based on Buddhist principles, and so, to prepare myself for this work, I enrolled for a course in Buddhism and meditation.

There are many forms and traditions of Buddhism, but underpinning all of them is a complex synthesis of philosophy, psychology and ethics, including a focus on the specific questions indicated above (as well as others) and culminating in the intensely practical issue: how should I conduct my life? And when the question is put like this, many of us, I think, would welcome 'helpful advice' of some sort. Who, we wonder, can give us advice on how to manage our lives (who to believe, what to believe in, what path to follow) and what sort of advice do we imagine it might be?

For example, how do we respond when we realise that political decisions are dictated not by considerations of ethics, justice or international law, but almost entirely by military and economic power strategies, or (at another level) by party advantage or personal self-interest? Knowing that news is now technically so easy to 'fake', and that government errors and deceptions are so routinely denied and covered up, how should we respond to those repeated calls for 'transparency' and 'trust'? Surrounded on every side and all the time by advertisements with the obviously delusional message that happiness arises from our acts of consumption, how can we judge what will *actually* bring us happiness? We are beleaguered by the multidimensional seductions of egotism (Note 1), even though most of us feel deep down that 'egotism' (whatever it is) cannot possibly be the basis for the life we would like to lead, especially in a society characterised by almost unbelievable extremes of wealth and poverty.

So we are stuck without any clear answers to such basic questions as: who are we? What are our obligations to others? What will bring us happiness? What do we want? What would be good for us? Where are we (the human race) headed? Not surprisingly, then, reports of *an epidemic of 'depression'* are frequent headline news, analysing the possible origins and meanings of widespread anxiety, fear, grief, remorse and guilt (Note 2). But however we interpret such reports, they contribute to our sense that there must be 'something more than this'; that something needs to change. But what? And how?

Why Buddhism?

The 'helpful advice' presented in this book is from a Tibetan Buddhist tradition. It can of course be argued that the world's religions all provide 'helpful advice' concerning precisely the questions outlined above, and that their teachings and their more or less universally proclaimed values ('love', 'generosity', etc.) also entail key elements of philosophy, ethics and psychology. I am happy to accept such arguments and I very much hope that Christians, Jews, Moslems, Hindus and Sikhs (as well as secularists and humanists) will all enjoy and value this book. However, religions are also *communities* bound together by observances (e.g. rules concerning food, drink and sex) and rituals. Indeed, the etymological root meaning of 'religion' is that it 'binds' people together. But rituals and observances not only bind one religious group together; they also serve to identify and *exclude* others who are not 'bound into' the religion or who are bound into a different religion. Traditional forms of Buddhism also involve ritual observances, but the appeal of Buddhism for westerners is that these rituals are not always of central importance, to the extent that that some would argue that Buddhism is a tradition of teachings, but *not* necessarily always 'a religion' (Note 3). Because of this, Buddhist teachings often seem to have a quality of 'anti-dogmatic' openness, and it is this that gives them an appeal beyond the Buddhist community.

One of the ways in which Buddhism is arguably not a religion is that we are not asked to believe that the truths of Buddhist teachings are definitively *revealed* in sacred texts. Texts exist of course, and key texts are studied with great care, but the truth of what they teach is only to be found in our own *experience* if we properly follow their guidance. In quite a modern way, therefore, Buddhism expresses a sort of pragmatism. In a well-known story, we are told that the teachings are like logs and pieces of wood by the side of a river that bars our path: but for them to be of any value we need to put them to practical use, by assembling them into a raft so that we can cross the river (i.e.from ignorance to understanding).

Another reason why Buddhism is often contrasted with other religions is that its teachings do not include a metaphysical, supernatural Creator. On the contrary, the traditional accounts of the Buddha's teachings suggest, in this respect, a sort of critical scepticism: that we cannot possibly have any well-founded *knowledge* concerning the nature of any such a Divine Agent or even whether such a Divine Agent exists or not. For this reason, the Buddhist notion of 'faith' is more like a feeling of confidence in the helpfulness of the traditional teachings than any sort of acceptance of theological arguments concerning the nature and existence of God. This gives Buddhism a widespread contemporary appeal: it does not seem to compete with other faiths nor with humanism, secularism or scientific theory, (there are even

Jewish Buddhists, humanist Buddhists and Buddhist Quakers, for example). And so the Buddhist teachings seem to allow us to focus on the nature of the reality that we, as human beings, *experience*, rather than on the nature of any Divine, 'Absolute' or 'Ultimate' Reality, although for many Buddhists this remains a contentious issue (Note 4).

Along with these elements of pragmatism and anti-metaphysical scepticism, there is a third key feature that makes Buddhist teachings attractive as responses to the various moral predicaments posed by the contemporary world, and this brings us back to Buddhism's implicit synthesis of philosophy, psychology, and ethics, previously mentioned.

The Buddhist tradition has almost always emphasised the central importance of compassionate engagement with the well-being of others. But this is not just an *ethical* injunction; it follows from the key teaching that our individual self is not a separate, fixed 'thing' but a continuously developing *process* in a universe entirely consisting of innumerable interlocking and interacting processes. Thus, we all consist of, for example, the microscopic and biological processes that keep us alive, and we are also involved in large-scale ecological systems and socio-cultural institutions such as families and communities.

Hence, when we interpret our experience simply from our own individualistic standpoint, (i.e. with ourselves – *our* concerns, *our* purposes – always at the centre) this is always an erroneous *philosophical* understanding. We always need to understand who we are and 'what' we are, in terms of our relationship with other beings and the rest of the natural world. For this reason, 'wisdom' concerning who we are as individuals is inseparable from 'compassion', i.e. experiencing ourselves as inextricably bound in sympathy to others. So, from a Buddhist perspective, to lack compassion is a form of misunderstanding, and to respond compassionately to a situation is to respond 'wisely'. (What we usually mean by 'wise' and wisdom' is worth pondering, of course!)

19

The link in Buddhist teachings between *psychology* and *ethics* is equally illuminating. It starts from the observation that we always respond to our experiences (our perceptions and also our feelings) with a momentary impulse that is either positive or negative, and it is this initial impulse that leads on to positive or negative states of mind. These states of mind (including feelings) tend to become habitual or long-lasting aspects of our being, and play an important part in defining our identity. However, they always start with momentary impulses, and these impulses can be noticed and interrupted, so that we always have the freedom to *choose* a creative *ethical* response, rather than merely *reacting* (i.e. spontaneously) (Note 5). In this way, what looks at first like a simple point concerning the 'psychology of perception' also has important ethical implications and possibilities.

And when these lines of argument are placed in the context of the important Buddhist teaching that all the phenomena of our experience are continuously changing (the doctrine of 'impermanence'), what emerges from the tradition is an emphasis on our human capacity for positive transformation, both personal and cultural.

Spirituality

At this point, I can imagine some readers saying, 'This is all very well, but couldn't most of this be equally well applied to humanism? Surely Buddhism, if not always a religion, is surely always a tradition of spirituality? If these fifty-nine pieces of advice represent a form of *Buddhist* teaching, should they not also include a clearly 'spiritual' element?

Quite true, but this raises the interesting question of what we mean by 'spirituality'. In a religious context, the term usually refers to a belief in a metaphysical level of being, in the 'soul', for example, as the 'divine essence' of the human individual, through which we can understand our lives in terms of Divine purposes. We might at the very least agree that to lead a 'spiritual' life is to seek the meaning and purpose of our lives in something or other that is external to and larger than our individuality. And usually, the spiritual life is thought to involve engaging in an effort to transcend our mundane motives and perceptions by applying our understanding of a Divine Will to the circumstances of our individual lives.

In Buddhism, there is indeed a contrast between the mundane as a state of relative ignorance and the spiritual as a state of larger understanding that transcends our everyday awareness, but it does not start out from a supernatural Divinity or the 'essence', divine or otherwise, of the human individual. The Buddhist teaching, mentioned previously, that all phenomena are in a continuous process of change, suggests that human beings also are continuously changing phenomena linked with all the other mutually transforming processes of the universe. This implies that an individual does not possess an unchanging, 'immortal' soul, but it also suggests that there *is* indeed a spiritual / transcendent dimension to our lives as soon as we become aware that we exist in a state of what we might call 'interbeing' (Note 6). The term is taken from the Vietnamese Buddhist teacher Thich Nath Hanh. It suggests how a sense of compassion, responsibility and openness arises when we recognise that as human beings we are inseparably bound into processes of mutual dependence and continuous change along with *all* other phenomena and beings. (Think of the countless chains of causality that have come to fruition, as it were, in your current action of reading this book, and also the impact of your own actions and words on everything and everyone you have ever come into contact with).

For Buddhism, spiritual awareness entails a full understanding of this teaching and trying to apply it continuously to our interactions with others. Its opposite – the Buddhist version of mundane ignorance – is the erroneous misunderstanding that we are entirely separate individuals, carelessly assuming that the immediate impression of our individual separateness that arises from our spontaneous experience is all the understanding we need. Put quite simply, therefore, for Buddhism a lack of 'spiritual' awareness is manifested in all the many forms of our egocentrism, and our spiritual development is expressed in a) our continuous questioning and curtailing of our egotistical impulses, and, b) increasing depth and effortlessness in our empathy with, and compassion for, the suffering of other beings. This interpretation of 'spirituality', as the opposite of our spontaneous, mundane egotism, is one way of expressing the key insight into the nature of our experience that (as we are told in the very earliest stories) the Buddha realised at the moment when he finally understood that he had discovered new and important truths to communicate to humanity (Note 7).

We might also say that our spirituality is engaged when we include and synthesise *all* the multifarious aspects of our being, and, in particular, when we experience the mysteriousness of being deeply moved – in our feelings, our bodily sensations and in our thinking – in ways that surprise us with an intensity that seems to defy any full explanation – e.g. our responses to music, dancing, poetry, or landscape.

In principle, nothing in this insight of the Buddha or in the teachings of the various religions need preclude adherents of Christianity, Judaism, Islam, Hinduism and even Humanists from saying, 'Well, if you put it like that, of course: me too!' And if this is your response: fine, read on, enjoy! However, it is important to note that Buddhist teachings are not just concerned with ideas (what we might call 'beliefs') but with the activities, usually called 'practices' that underpin and enact them. What the Buddha realised was the importance and effectiveness of a certain type of practice. And the fifty-nine slogans are above all helpful suggestions about what to DO.

The *Practice* of Meditation

In 1995, I received an invitation to visit Thailand in order to work with a Thai colleague in devising methods of social research based on Buddhist principles. How interesting, I thought. So in October I joined a group of about twenty people on a short 'Introduction to Buddhism' course in the basement of a large old house that in those days was home to the Cambridge Buddhist Centre. By the end of the course, I was fascinated by the teachings and their implications. But what seemed particularly important and surprisingly helpful was a very new and different *practical experience*: sitting still and concentrating on my breathing; paying careful attention to the thoughts that from time to time interrupted the sequence of breaths and responding to these thoughts by 'letting them go', so that they did *not* drag me into my usual daydreams, memories, and anxieties – in other words, the *practice* of 'meditation'. After twenty minutes or so of sitting and focusing on my breathing in this way, I was amazed to discover (repeatedly, on each evening of the course) that I felt both more energised and more tranquil.

The practice of meditation is one of the central activities of Buddhism. It is one of the three pathways to (or aspects of) 'wisdom' – that elusive but all-inclusive term summarising the ideal of so much human activity. The other two, alongside meditation, are, firstly, reading and studying and, secondly, reflection – the process of understanding, questioning and integrating the many facets of our experience. Meditation can take a number of different forms, but the breathing practice that I initially encountered (combining detailed awareness and intense concentration) is perhaps the most basic. Visualisation (of a sequence of relationships, for example) and the recitation of mantras are also frequently involved, and in some traditions (including Jewish, Hindu, Christian and Sufi) chanting. But, especially in Buddhism, from the earliest times, paying careful attention to the breath has been a key element of meditation, as it is indeed in the teaching of the Fifty-Nine Slogans presented in this book. Continuously involving the breath is an important method of ensuring that our meditation is genuinely a practice of 'engaging with' our experience and not just a process of 'thinking about' it. Historically, the word 'breath' is linked to 'spirit' (Latin: 'spiritus') and one dictionary meaning of spirit is 'the breath of life'.

The particular meditation practice presented in the Fifty-nine Slogans is traditionally described as a process of 'mind training', and the term is another reminder that meditation is above all an *activity*. We 'train' in an activity or 'practice' to develop our ability, become *more* expert, *more* skilful at it –

the analogy with engaging in sport and music spring immediately to mind. And this is an indicator that in meditation we are concerned with *changing* who we are (our thinking, our feelings, our words and our actions) through a process of *sustained effort.*

So, what sort of change do we want to achieve through this sustained effort? Although 'mind-training' is the usual translation, as with all Buddhist meditation, much more than the mind is involved. The purpose of the Fifty-nine slogans is to 'train' the mind to understand the whole of our experience – to understand ourselves (our motives, our impulses); to understand our interactions with family and friends; to understand our responses to strangers, colleagues and even opponents, and how we experience the various forms and degrees of suffering that we encounter: the break-up of a relationship, bereavement, ageing, and the prospect of our unpredictable, always potentially imminent death. And finally, as a result of this change in our self-understanding, to replace the way we act in our everyday lives with more helpful, more sensitive, more 'compassionate' responses to others.

To encompass all this implies more than 'the mind', and more than what we usually mean by 'understanding'. In practising meditation, we not only attempt to engage with our awareness of what is going on in our minds, but our awareness of the whole of our being (Note 8). Thus, practising meditation includes a movement of our feelings, an awakening of our heart and our imagination, an expansion of our appreciation of beauty in its various forms, a deepening of our empathy, and a broadening of our consciousness to include the whole of the world we inhabit.

This may seem rather a lot – daunting even – but the basic point really is that to meditate is to engage seriously and in a practical way with our deepest values and with a more authentic, more comprehensive, less ego-centred, and more integrated sense of who we are and who we could be. For most of us this is not a search for 'perfection' (whatever that might be!) but for progress. And in hoping that our efforts will lead to some sort of progress, no matter how slow, we can take encouragement from the traditional texts reporting that The Buddha continued to meditate throughout his life, long after the moment of his initial 'Awakening' (See note 7).

Why Slogans? (And How to Use Them)

The origin of the Tibetan mind-training practice is traditionally attributed to the work of the teachers Atisha and Chekawa in the 11th and 12th centuries respectively. The original fragmentary 'lines' of the teaching are called 'slogans' by the influential contemporary teachers and commentators Chogyam Trungpa and Pema Chodron. Some may feel that 'slogans' is an inappropriate term, given its association with advertising and political campaigning. But it is difficult to think of an alternative: 'mottos', for example, reminds one of Christmas crackers, and 'maxims' seems rather pretentious; whereas 'slogans' seems after all, in the contemporary world, nicely ironic. So I have preferred to follow the example of Trungpa and Chodron.

These 'lines' or 'slogans' are usually presented under seven very general headings as 'The Seven Points of Mind Training' (Note 9). However, the fifty-nine 'lines' (i.e. the slogans) are the original elements, and this is important because unlike most other sets of teachings they are not presented in the form of a unified analytical or narrative structure. Rather, in the words of Thupten Jinpa, one of the most recent and authoritative translators, 'Every single line can be seen as encapsulating the entire teaching...' (Note 10).

This does not mean that the slogans merely repeat one another. Rather, the relationship between them is expressed by the poetic image in the traditional text describing Indra's net. Above the palace belonging to the mythical figure of Indra there was suspended a jewelled net, in which at each intersection of its strands there were jewels that reflected all the other jewels at all the other intersections. This image can be seen as expressing an important aspect of Buddhist teachings – that they form a closely interlocking pattern without being sequential or linear. Hence, the Buddha is reported as saying that it was possible to gain an understanding of the teachings as a whole by contemplating deeply and comprehensively just a single one of the teachings. And it doesn't matter which one: the Buddha is also reported as explaining that he has given 84,000 different teachings because everyone (i.e. all 84,000 of us!) has had a different life experience, and therefore, we each need our own individual starting point from which to begin our understanding and our practice.

This suggests an important practical consequence of the slogan format. Chogyam Trungpa suggests that each slogan can be thought of as a 'reminder' (Note 11), and this in turn emphasises that meditation involves regular and frequent repetition, so that it can gradually become adapted to our own personal circumstances.

In this way we take full advantage of the slogan form of the teachings, where each 'slogan-element' reflects and illuminates the others. Our practice therefore no longer arises from a body of teachings that we simply *follow*. Rather, the teachings exist as a set of possibilities that requires us to *improvise* a sense of their coherence. The randomisation process means that our meditation practice can be guided by the tradition of the teachings but at the same time we have the opportunity to build up our individual version of the practice, as a gradually accumulating synthesis, by working on our experience first with one of slogans and then with a quite different one, and in the end with all of them.

Pema Chodron explains the method of using the slogans as follows: each day one of the slogans is chosen at random as a reminder to focus on that particular aspect of the teachings, although of course – following the image of Indra's net – all aspects reflect every other aspect. And the following day we go on to another reminder – another slogan – also chosen at random (Note 12). Although the books by Chogyam Trungpa and Pema Chodron both contain quite elaborate commentaries on the slogans, the presentation of the slogans themselves is also 'randomised' by being printed onto a set of cards. The cards are then shuffled and one card is drawn for the day, indicating which of the slogans is going to be the focus for the day's meditation practice. In this book, in contrast, the randomisation of the practice is made possible by printing the slogans on separate pages. (This is further explained below.)

The framework of the overall teachings is presented in the first ten slogans, which are usually grouped together under the headings 'The Preliminaries' and 'The Main Practice'. But the way some of them are phrased requires rather a lot of explanation, especially for readers without prior experience of Buddhism or meditation. So, whereas slogans 11–59 are presented individually, so that we can work with them using the 'random' process outlined above, these first ten slogans are not presented separately but are combined into the conventional format of a connected explanation. This is divided into two sections: 'The Preliminaries' (including slogan 1), presented in Part Two) and 'The Main Practice', (slogans 2–10), presented in Part Three.

In Part Four, each of the remaining slogans is printed on a separate page together with a brief explanation intended to clarify its meaning as a free-standing statement that also, in some way, reflects the teachings as a whole.

In order to select a slogan from Part Four at random, use the index of the slogans on page 72 Choose a particular slogan by closing your eyes and pointing at the page. Then turn to the page number closest to your finger to see which slogan is indicated as the focus for the next phase of your meditation. (Or you can simply flick the pages to see which slogan comes up.) Then take that slogan as a guide for your meditation (in the light of the outline of the teachings presented in the first two sections) for a day or two, and then select another slogan, again at random. In this way, the slogan method suggests that the practice of meditation can be (or even *needs* to be) thought of as a process of *gradual self-education.*

All this is a reminder that, as mentioned earlier, repetition is an essential element of the practice of meditation (as it is in 'practicing' the violin or 'practicing' a tennis serve). The slogan format simply makes this explicit, and provides a method for maintaining one's motivation to meditate by regularly adding a new element. This means that if you are convinced by this book, you will NOT think, at the end, 'Oh this is an interesting book; I must add it to the shelf where I keep my other 'interesting' books. Rather you will keep it readily to hand, as a user's manual – like a pocket toolkit, or a box of tissues!

Gurus and Friends: Whose Advice to Follow?

Despite the long tradition behind the teachings, there are differences between the versions of the various Tibetan commentators, in terms of the way some of the slogans are translated and explained, and also differences in interpretation. For example, one writer (universally respected in the tradition) makes a very clear distinction between two of the slogans, while another writer (also very influential) suggests that those two slogans have roughly the same meaning but that this does not really matter (Note 13).There are also slight differences in the order in which the slogans are listed and how they are grouped under the mind training headings (Note 14). However, the differences of interpretation between the various Tibetan versions are minor, and the challenge of transposing the teachings from their original Tibetan setting to a version attuned to modern western culture turned out to be difficult but not insuperable.

But there was one issue which seemed unavoidably to require quite a radical reinterpretation, namely the role of 'the guru' in learning and practising meditation. In Tibetan Buddhism, the teacher (the guru) is the paramount authority, guaranteeing, without any possibility of dispute, the authenticity and validity of the teaching. His authority derives ultimately from his 'lineage' – the long chain of ordinations linking one's own contemporary guru to an original master, who lived perhaps centuries previously. (Rather like the 'apostolic succession' in Catholicism.)

The idea that the authority of someone's knowledge and skill derives from the ancient tradition of which he or she is the current representative is a central part of the culture of feudal societies such as classical Tibet. But this model of cultural authority plays little part in modern western society. In liberal democracies, authority is supposed to be derived either from a *legal* document (e.g. a university degree certifying your professional accreditation) or from the *rational* arguments you put forward to justify your point of view. (Hence the importance of 'debating' in the process of government.) Indeed, in liberal democracies, the term 'guru' is often used almost ironically. So I seemed at first to have hit a major problem when I discovered that the texts all insisted that one's 'guru' is to be treated with unquestioning submission and devotion, not only in the commentaries on the teachings but in the actual wording of one or two of the slogans.

Fortunately, however, there is another powerful term we can use here instead, namely 'friendship'. The idea of friendship plays a key role in the early Buddhist teachings and in Buddhist practice generally. What is meant is a form of 'spiritual friendship' – a phrase describing *both* the mutual care and respect between a teacher and a student *and also* the relationship between people who share a commitment to a path of ethical and spiritual development through their practice of awareness, understanding and meditation. The same term can be applied to both roles (Note 15). In the Tibetan classical tradition the feelings we have towards a teacher who inspires us can be listed as follows: trust, commitment, gratitude, admiration (for their wisdom and insight), and willingness to learn from them when these insights *challenge* our understanding or our actions (Note 16). But we, as westerners, might agree that this list could equally well describe for us an ideal of 'serious' friendship – a small group of people we know well – not just those we might conventionally call friends, but including, for example, perhaps, a partner, a brother or sister, or a neighbour – people we admire and whose values we share. Meeting and talking with them provides us with support, guidance, helpful criticism and companionship, and we do the same for them.

This might also suggest that it could be useful to use the book in conjunction with three or four friends, by meeting up for discussion and perhaps to meditate together. Many people find that meditating in the company with others is very helpful and so it might be worth putting some effort into finding 'partners' for this. Groups and meetings like this could be thought of as offering a process of mutual or reciprocal support – resembling perhaps a sort of 'group counselling'.

And so, to return finally to the question posed by the title of this section: one of the early Buddhist texts tells the following story. The Buddha arrived at a small town, preceded by his reputation as the most insightful thinker of the era. A group of townspeople came to see him and complained that a whole succession of different philosophers and religious teachers had visited the town, each proclaiming the correctness of their own doctrines and rubbishing the ideas of everyone else. How, they said, do we know what to believe or whose advice to follow?

The Buddha replied: 'You are quite right; this is indeed a very important question. To begin with, don't accept someone's teaching because of the teacher's reputation, because of the teacher's lineage, because of the cleverness of his reasoning, or because he happens to be your teacher. There are only two things to take notice of. Firstly, whether or not you feel, from your experience, that these teachings will lead you into greed, hatred and delusion, and therefore into harm and suffering or whether they will lead you into their opposites – kindliness, honesty and happiness. The second thing to notice is whether these teachings are praised or rejected by those whom you consider to be wise. (It is interesting, however, that the Buddha's advice still leaves us with the difficult but helpful question: how do we decide who, exactly, is 'wise'?)

*****

Notes for Part One

1) The problem of 'egotism' is of crucial importance throughout the teachings, and it has many dimensions. I have tended to use the term 'egotism' for the sake of simplicity, but this can seem to limit the meaning to everyday selfishness. In some ways 'egoism', meaning 'mistakenly or carelessly taking oneself to be the centre of the world,' would be more accurate. Other terms that are equally relevant are, for example: ego-promotion, ego cherishing, 'ego-clinging', ego-centric, self-important, self-congratulatory, and self-aggrandising.

2) Just by typing 'Epidemic of Depression' into an internet search-engine, we are presented with an array of reports, from academic journals and, for example, the United Nations; including discussions as to what 'depression' consists of and whether the evidence shows that there is currently more of it, or merely a greater awareness, and whether or not its symptoms have recently become more acute.

3) For example, Trevor Ling; *The Buddha*, Penguin, 1973; Stephen Batchelor: *Buddhism Without Beliefs,* Bloomsbury, 1998.

4) See <http//jayarava.blogspot.com/2017/02/ experience & reality.html>

5) See Sangharakshita: 'The Reactive Mind and the Creative Mind', in *A Guide to the Buddhist Path*, Windhorse Publications, 1990, pp. 71-2.

6) This term, which I find very beautiful in itself and in its implications, was coined by Thich Nhat Hanh, in his book *Being Peace,* Rider, 1987, chapter six.

7) This moment of realisation is called the Buddha's 'awakening'; hence his title 'The Buddha', meaning 'The Awakened One'.

8) The Sanskrit word '*citta*' (pronounced 'chitta') is used to describe this inclusive model of our being. It is useful because, unlike any English equivalent, it

refs *equally* to the emotional and the cognitive / intellectual dimension of our experience and our activity.

9) The 'seven points' are given as follows, although translations vary slightly: i) The Preliminary Reminders; ii) The Main Practice; iii) Learning Positively from Adverse Circumstances; iv) Practising Mind Training in Everyday Life; v) Evaluating Progress; vi) Commitments of Mind Training; vii) Guidelines for Mind Training.

10) *Mind Training, The Great Collection*, Trans. Thupten Jinpa Wisdom Publications, 2006, Introduction, p. 5

11) Chogyam Trungpa: *Training the Mind and Cultivating Loving Kindness,* Shambala, 1993, p.57

12) Pema Chodron: Introduction to Chogyam Trungpa: op.cit., p..ix

13) Compare Jamgon Kongtrul: op.cit. (below), p.32 with Chogyam Trungpa: op.cit., p.93

14) List of translations and commentators consulted:
Chogyam Trungpa: *Training the Mind and Cultivating Loving Kindness,* Shambala, 1993
Pema Chodron: *Start Where You Are,* Shambala, 1994
Gomo Tulku: *Becoming a Child of the Buddhas,* Wisdom Publications, 1998
Khenchen Thrangu Rinpoche: *The Seven Points of Mind Training*, Namo Buddha Publications, 2004
Jamgon Kongtrul: *The Great path of Awakening,* Shambala, 2005
Geshe Jampa Tegchok: *The Kindness of Others,*
Lama Yeshe Wisdom Archive, 2006
Thupten Jinpa: *Mind Training, The Great Collection,* Wisdom Publications, 2006

15) See Sangharakshita: *A Guide to the Buddhist Path,* Windhorse, 1996, p. 109;
p. 208. The term linking the role of spiritual teacher and spiritual friend is '*kalyana mitrata*'.

16) Chogyam Trungpa: op.cit: p. 106; Pema Chodron: op.cit.: p.135-7

Part Two:
Getting Started

Practising Meditation

Our first response when people give us 'helpful advice' is to think, and even perhaps to say: 'Easier said than done!' And rightly so, because changing our mind-set, let alone our behaviour, always requires more than 'saying', i.e. more than being *told about* some new fact or idea or possible line of action. And this is why the emphasis in Part One was that the teachings presented in the fifty-nine slogans describe a 'practice' – something that we each, individually, need to *do* (repeatedly); combining our feelings as well as our thinking, forming new habits (trying to let go of egotism, for example), and involving a concentrated awareness of our breathing. In other words: not just 'receiving advice' but 'practicing meditation'.

I hope that Part One has succeeded in making the point that something along the lines of this process of meditation could well be beneficial (in terms of our attempts to live well in a difficult world!). But as yet it will probably have seemed to many readers (especially those who have not yet engaged in anything they think of as 'meditation') to be rather complex and unfamiliar. So before going any further it is worth noting, in straightforward terms, what 'practicing' meditation entails.

The first thing is to find a place where we can sit quietly and concentrate. To begin with, this is likely to be just a corner in a room, and we might symbolise the tranquillity we are hoping for with a flower or a candle. Also, in order to concentrate we need to be free from any distracting discomfort in the way we are sitting, and this will mean sitting in a straight-backed chair rather than an armchair and finding a comfortable upright posture, neither leaning forwards nor leaning back.

But we mustn't get too rigid about this, because we want meditation to have a beneficial effect in our lives generally. So we would hope that after a few weeks of practicing our meditation in our special corner we will also be capable of finding a tranquil 'space' in our minds whenever we really need it: caught in a traffic jam, for example, or on the telephone, listening for the twentieth time to a recorded voice saying, 'Your call is very important to us'.

We need to remember that meditating is *not* the same as 'thinking about' something. Thinking about something easily starts to go round in circles – a process of pondering or brooding, that can increase our anxiety without shedding much light on the topic of our thoughts. The main 'action' of meditation, in contrast, is concentrating as hard as we can on a particular aspect of our awareness – sounds, for example, or physical sensations, or, in particular, our breathing. Concentrating intensely on our breathing, noticing the satisfying rhythm of the in-breath followed by the out-breath, is one of the main traditional methods used to try to bring peace and quiet to our state of mind and thus to deflect our attention from what we would otherwise be tempted to 'think about'.

So, concentrating our awareness is the starting point of meditation. And 'awareness' includes our physical sensations, our breathing and also our concerns and the state of our feelings. We try to become aware of, for example, whether we are feeling relaxed or anxious, energetic or lethargic, sad or contented, peaceful or irritated.

But sometimes, starting by concentrating on our concerns and feelings can generate such an unstable, 'speedy' state of mind that it prevents us from letting go the anxieties or plans or memories that are currently dominating our lives. When we find this happening, an effective strategy is to aid our concentration on our breathing by *counting* each breath, going from 'one' to 'ten' and starting again at 'one' whenever we lose count.)

This leads to another very important general aspect of meditation: we are trying to develop a state of mind that is in our own terms more 'positive', e.g. more relaxed, kinder, less irritable, more 'in control' of our feelings, more energetically involved with people, etc. And we are trying to cultivate this more positive state of mind not just on a single occasion but as a habit.

Hence the important point, already mentioned, that learning to meditate always involves repetition, i.e. 'practice' in the sense used in sports training and learning a musical instrument. This also means that meditation always has at some level a sense of *purpose*, as well as a sense of *accepting* and appreciating experience as we find it.

But this does not mean that in meditating we are conscious of *striving* towards a goal (i.e. 'the person I would like to be'). This may be present for us as an underlying, background motive, and perhaps it needs to be. But during meditation itself our awareness is a focus on exploring and enjoying our concentration on the present, so that we find ourselves so strongly aware of the present moment that our anxieties about the past and the future temporarily drop away.

Meditation is often described as 'following a path' towards this more positive state of being that we can imagine for ourselves. This helpfully suggests that our progress (along the path) can be (and usually is) gradual and not necessarily rapid. But it would be a mistake to infer that the qualities we are seeking to develop constitute a *distant* goal, because the traditional teaching is that the qualities we need are already within us, as our deepest potential. Our gradual progress in the practice of meditation, therefore, is better thought of as a gradual removal of errors and confusions. (In some traditional texts the process is described as being rather like removing the mud encrusting a precious jewelled ornament that we possess but which we have forgotten and has become buried in the earth!)

As further practical guidance, on pages 69-71 there are some detailed explanations of how to use the slogans in the randomised way previously described, based on examples from my own experience of using the slogans to support my own meditation.

Slogan 1: "First Train in the Preliminaries"

Reflecting on 'The Preliminaries'

Although meditation needs to be clearly distinguished from 'thinking', it is quite closely associated with a process that we might call 'reflection' – calling to mind aspects of the traditional teachings and also the whole range of our knowledge and understanding concerning the disparate, often contradictory aspects of our experience; seeking anew our sense of coherence, our deepest values and aspirations. Whereas the *practice* of meditation is a form of concentrated awareness, the *practice* of reflection (differentiating it from merely 'thinking') is a process of questioning and challenging our spontaneous responses (both our thoughts and our feelings). Working with the slogans always involves both 'meditating' *and* 'reflecting' on our experience so that in practical terms we don't need to worry overmuch about the distinction, as long as we make sure that we don't lapse into just 'thinking'.

We can see this as soon as we look at the very first slogan, which is intended to get us started by introducing us to 'The 'Preliminaries' by means of 'The Four Reminders'. They are called 'reminders' because they refer to aspects of our experience which, although they immediately challenge us to reflect on some of our most urgent and important issues, are in themselves so familiar as to be almost self-evident. These are listed below, including a brief explanatory paragraph. Taken together, they give us a helpful and comprehensive point of departure, and they also illustrate how working with the slogans involves awareness of our feelings as well as challenging our thinking, i.e. the practice of meditating and at the same time the practice of reflecting.

The Four Reminders

First: *Be grateful for the precious gift of being born as a human being.*

At one level this 'reminder' arises from a long tradition of belief that human beings who lead unethical lives can be reborn as, say, spiders or jackals. This concern with a favourable or unfavourable rebirth is for many of us alien or at least not particularly illuminating. On the other hand it probably *is* helpful to remember that, uniquely among other living species, we human beings have the remarkable opportunity of having the *freedom to reflect* on the nature (or what we might call the 'meaning') of our existence: not just who we are but what we are, how we came to 'be', our past and our potential. This imaginative ability to understand ourselves in a variety of different ways (and thus to envisage changing ourselves) not only sets us apart from other forms of life but provides us with a sense that our lives have varied and interesting possibilities. It is important to remember this with gratitude when from time to time we feel *burdened* by our freedom, by the very scope of our choices, and feel tempted to envy what we take to be the simple tranquillity of life as a tree or a cat.

Second: *Life inevitably ends in death, and we never know when or how.*

As a piece of general advice, this is so familiar that we are in danger of taking it for granted and ignoring it. (In modern society death is so much out of sight it is usually also 'out of mind', and certainly not a regular aspect of our practical awareness: of course, we don't want to be 'morbid'.) But ultimately there is no point in suppressing our awareness that finally, as we know perfectly well, we will be forced to 'deal with' death, So what could be more important and helpful than to practice in advance incorporating into our experience the sense of fragility, precariousness and impermanence that death as an inescapable event imposes? And let us not delay or procrastinate: death can occur without warning – while we are running a half-marathon or driving home from work. On the other hand, we want to avoid 'undue anxiety'. What we mean by 'undue' is of course a big question, but what we can say is that it is helpful for each of us to work in our own way on *accepting* our fragility and impermanence as the way things are, the way *we* are. In the end, death shapes all our experience, and reminds us that we need to hold lightly to whatever as individuals we *possess* (wealth, status, power. etc.), precisely because they are things that we are inevitably going to *lose.* Better therefore not to cling too closely to any aspect of our lives that could be thought of as a 'lose-able' possession, and to consider carefully what other purposes and sources of meaning might be available to us.

Third: *'Karma': All our actions have consequences for good or for harm*

All events, including our own actions, create an endless chain of consequences, and this creates a strong *ethical* significance for any event that we in some way *intend* (i.e. as opposed to mere 'accidents'). Sometimes, the importance of *intention* in the notion of karma is ignored, suggesting that the various causes of an event can always be analysed in such a way as to *blame* someone or other. Our intended actions (including our thoughts and words) do indeed create chains of consequences which are so long and complicated that we can never know when or where someone may have experienced something unfortunate as a result of our actions. But this does not imply that anyone is necessarily to *blame*; rather, that in any situation we need to be aware of our freedom to act one way or another and that we therefore need to take responsibility for our choices. So it is always helpful to reflect how in a given situation there might have been a possibility that we have not yet considered: how we could have behaved more ethically, and what we might do now for the best. In this way the title of this reminder, can help us consider our actions in a wider moral perspective.

Fourth: *Human experience often involves some degree of suffering.*

Easily forgotten – especially if we are particularly lucky, optimistic, egotistical or thoughtless! But such forgetfulness, although it may look at first like quite a successful way of coping, is a failure to *understand* how 'suffering' is a key parameter of our existence. Sometimes suffering can be minimal, e.g. a tinge of regret that no experience ever quite lives up to our anticipation of it. Sometimes it is the straightforward sorrow at our mortality. Sometimes it is the anguish that arises when we fully experience the impermanence of everything we hold dear. Sometimes it is when we are struck by the mystery concerning the how and why of our existence, by our apparently inevitable ignorance. But in any case, this aspect of our experience challenges us to try to understand the nature of pain as part of our humanity and the place of our own pain and happiness in the context of everything else.

Part Three:
The Main Practice

A Summary of the Basic Teachings

Atisha's fifty-nine slogans present a specific tradition of meditation practice, which is particularly attractive in its down-to-earth practicality, its ironic humour, and its unique method of presentation based on the 'open' choice of slogans. But the apparent openness of the fifty-nine slogans can seem rather bewildering, not to say mysterious, unless we start off by establishing a firm grasp of the initial teachings, as presented in the first ten slogans. The first slogan, 'Always Train in the Preliminaries' with its 'Four Reminders' (see Part Two), enables us to start from quite a familiar level of awareness. But the next few slogans (2–10), traditionally given the title of 'The Main Practice', do require some explanation.

So, in Part Three, slogans 2–10 are amplified and combined into an account of the basic teachings that underlie this traditional method of meditation, in order to provide a context and a starting point for using the rest of slogans 11–59 (listed separately in Part Four). The slogans that constitute this 'Main Practice' (what we might call 'the basic teachings') are listed on page 65 in the traditional order. In order to clarify the underlying structure of the teachings the following summary is arranged under four headings, as follows:

First, there is a challenge to our understanding of the world as we experience it – *Accept the 'emptiness' of our experience* (slogans 2, 4 and 6).

Second there is a challenge to our self-awareness – *Appreciate the open, all-inclusive foundation of our being* (slogans 3 and 5).

Third there is a radical challenge to our emotional responses – *Recognise the necessity of compassion* (slogans 7 and 8).

Finally, there is an equally radical challenge to the way we relate to others – *Avoid the 'poison' arising from the delusions of the ego* (slogan 9).

This four-fold emphasis may initially suggest that when we are using the slogan format these different aspects need to be distinguished. This can indeed be a helpful starting point, but in the end all four aspects combine to form a single coherent vision of a radical ideal for human interaction.

Accept the 'Emptiness' of Our Experience

The slogans present this teaching by suggesting that our experiences are, in the traditional term, 'empty', and like dreams or illusions. At first this seems oddly unconvincing. We feel we can readily differentiate between, on the one hand, our dreams and illusions and, on the other hand our 'normal' experiences, which we take to be 'real' The term 'empty' comes as a further shock, and immediately suggests two questions: 'What are our experiences supposed to be *empty* of?' and 'Why is it important that we become aware of this *emptiness*?'

The first question is less shocking when we interpret it in terms of the fairly familiar idea that our experiences are always, in the end, subjective manifestations of our mind rather than solid objective facts firmly grounded in an external reality. So we might be inclined to substitute the less worrying term 'insubstantial' for 'empty'. The key point here is that our experiences can never be 'objective' or 'firmly grounded' in an external reality because our access to any external reality can never be direct but, on the contrary, must always take place indirectly through the medium of our experience itself – our senses, our feelings, our thoughts, etc. So we cannot make a final or certain decision about some aspect of the world we live in simply by holding up a mirror to Nature (to echo the title of an influential argument by the philosopher Richard Rorty (Note 1). A mirror of this kind does not and cannot exist. Instead, all we can do to investigate our experience is to ask questions and engage carefully in conversations about it with others.

At one level this may, initially, seem obvious – merely echoing a fairly familiar philosophical idea. Familiar in a sense perhaps, but nevertheless challenging. Precisely because most of us most of the time think and act as though we do indeed have direct access to an external objective reality. Yes, at one level we do know how difficult it is to be 'impartial' or 'accurate' or 'certain' in making a decision about some aspect of the world: 'What is going on here?' 'Why did that happen?' 'Why do I feel like this?' But in the end we routinely make an implicit claim to be in possession of 'objective facts in the real world' that prove with certainty that our view of the matter is the correct one. (As in the commonly overheard: 'I completely understand your point of view, but the fact of the matter is…') Which is why instead of asking questions we make assertions, and conversations turn into arguments, and then into quarrels, and finally wars.

So, it is by continuously remembering, moment by moment, the insubstantiality (the 'emptiness') of all the phenomena of our experience that we can set aside the illusions of what we might call the 'culture of objective facts' in which we live, and recognise that things are *not* fixed, determined) or proved. On the contrary (to echo the work of another influential philosopher, Karl Popper, our current knowledge always has the status of a set of 'conjectures' awaiting possible refutation in the future (Note 2). Our minds don't simply *perceive* the world of our experience, by passively receiving images from our senses. Rather, we actively *construct* our world through continuous processes of remembering, comparing, considering, telling and listening to stories, and generally sharing and conversing. In this way each of the phenomena of our experience (objects, people, situations, feelings) may itself be thought of as a process – a process in the end of our own creation and interpretation, always changing in some way or other and always lacking in objective substance or essence, because everything in our experience is mediated by our understanding and by all the influences upon our understanding from the culture we live in.

Nevertheless, the fact that I have no direct access to an external reality other than through my experience (i.e. my interpretation of data provided by my sense organs) does not mean that there is no such thing as an external reality and that therefore we can do and think exactly as the whim takes us. On the contrary, the structure and methods of our reasoning certainly seem to have *some* sort of effective relationship with the structure and processes of the natural world; otherwise we would not be able to carry out heart surgery or to design aircraft that regularly and safely take off and land. Indeed, all our familiar experiences give us good reason to believe that there is something or other 'out there'; because any doubt on that score would leave us unable to carry on routine conversations with other people or to cross a road.

Once I can accept that my experiences are empty of an objective substance or essence I can also recognise that my experiences are not *separate* phenomena that can be comprehended in isolation from each other. My perception of each one is influenced by a whole range of interlocking factors, e.g. my up-bringing, my network of relationships, the structure and routines of my language, the mass media, and the history and politics of the state of which I am a citizen And these same influences condition my choices, my values, my opinions, and even, in the end, my experience of my mind and of my identity. So the further implication here is that although the world of our experience is not 'given' but 'constructed', we do not construct it on our own ('unaided', as it were) but collectively, interpersonally, communally, rather than individually (Note 3).

When we meditate, therefore, we start by understanding that we need to 'train' our minds by continuous attention and questioning in order to keep *reminding* ourselves of the insubstantiality ('emptiness') of our experiences. In some respects, as I have suggested, the theory underlying this insight is not unfamiliar, but to *experience* the truth of the theory is difficult, and it is difficult because at a common-sense level it is counterintuitive.

And this is where we realise that 'training our understanding' needs to involve the whole of our being, because it involves our emotions and our convictions. For example, we tend to cling quite emotionally to the sense of certainty arising from our belief that we are directly in contact with the facts of an external objective world. Sometimes this clinging to our certainties serves to reinforce our self-esteem, our belief in our superiority to others, or at least the superiority of our own opinions. But sometimes this same conviction that our opinions and emotions are firmly grounded in an external reality can be self-limiting, even self-destructive, by serving to reinforce negative images of ourselves and a sense that our problems are inevitable and perhaps insoluble.

In both cases (both the positive and the negative), our sense of certainty traps our understanding within what we take to be a fixed set of external conditions, and solidifies our views so that we find it difficult to recognise helpful alternatives. It is a radical challenge to these emotions and convictions to accept that our supposed certainties are not 'objectively' grounded and are always open to question and revision, and that we therefore need to treat them lightly and combine them with a willing scepticism.

But this scepticism requires delicate handling, because there are dangers lurking here. In focusing on the insubstantiality of *everything,* we may open ourselves to the feeling that because everything is 'empty' and nothing is 'real', nothing *matters*. At the heart of this danger is a Zen-like paradox, as follows. 'The mind thinking the thought, *Everything is insubstantial*, is also insubstantial'. And this may lead us to the unsettling thought that, 'If this *I* is insubstantial, perhaps no significance or value can be attached to any of its thinking or its actions.'

But do not fear; help is at hand! This same argument contains, as the slogan suggests (See slogan 4, below) its own 'antidote' and a solution. If insubstantiality characterises *all*

51

our experience, then the thought 'Everything is insubstantial' is itself also insubstantial and the whole argument is therefore self-cancelling: we can (and indeed should) treat all our thinking with a degree of scepticism, and this includes all the arguments of the previous paragraph. The threats they seem to pose are themselves not grounded objectively or externally and thus they do not, as we might initially think, lead us to despair. Rather, they are grounded, like everything else, in our own thinking, i.e. in our own emotions and choices and the culture that has shaped us. And so we can see them not as threats but as helpful challenges to our understanding.

The main challenge posed by accepting the insubstantiality of our experience, clearly, is to let go of our craving for certainty. But it is also an opportunity to see our activity as 'playful' – not in the sense of 'uncommitted' or 'not serious', but in the sense of: creative, open, explorative, and committed to new learning and development rather than to 'proving a point'. Such a general stance towards our activity, to our lives in fact, brings with it a liberating sense of hope, arising from a confidence that new interpretations of experience are always possible because current conditions are always impermanent and in process of changing. In this way, to accept fully the insubstantiality of our experiences is both a training of the mind in continuous self-questioning and an awakening of the heart to different possibilities of feeling.

Appreciate the Open, All-Inclusive Foundation of Our Being

So, how shall we seek this counter-intuitive acceptance of the insubstantiality of all our experience? What sort of effort and what sort of awareness would it entail?

The phrase 'the open, all-inclusive foundation of our being' does not trip easily off the tongue, to say the least, but we need to take careful notice of it since it evokes a crucially important but elusive aspect of the capacities and qualities that enable us to meditate (see slogan 5).

The open, all-inclusive foundation of our being is *crucially important* because this is where *all* our experience is present, where no aspect of our being is excluded; where we experience a sense of being in touch with something deep and heartfelt in our self-awareness, and a sense of self-acceptance (including the 'dark side' of our being).

And yet it is also *elusive*, because it especially involves 'letting go' – of thoughts, beliefs and judgements. It involves ceasing to run around after the endless circles of our thinking, and it involves experiencing the insubstantiality (the 'emptiness') of things, events and people, together with their inevitable impermanence. Also, the whole phrase – 'open', 'all-inclusive, 'foundation' – reminds us that this is more than just a process of reasoning. Rather, we try to let the thoughts that spring into our mind float away, creating for ourselves a 'space', where we can let go of links between our experiences and words or concepts, i.e. where we avoid identifying and labelling. Instead, our awareness is concentrated on, for example, the different phases of our breathing or other bodily sensations as they arise and cease. This involves a reduced awareness of our surroundings and thus both a sense of 'spaciousness' and of concentration. In the end, it may seem to involve a reduced awareness of our identity, and instead a radically transformed set of sensations, such as we might perhaps imagine to be the experience of dreaming or the experience of an infant in the womb. (See slogans 2 and 3). Experiencing this can involve a sudden sense that everything is slightly *unfamiliar,* as we focus with intense awareness on the detail of each successive moment with an open horizon of meaning.

All this sounds potentially rather unsettling. But we must not forget that becoming aware of this 'unconscious' foundation of our being is traditionally assumed to be positive: a state of mind and feeling where we experience a sense of relaxation, equanimity and, in the depths of our being, our capacity for openness, for clarity and for sensitivity (Note 4). In other words: our ability to *accept* and *welcome* our experience, our ability to understand a *coherent pattern* in our experience, and, perhaps most important of all, a sense of *empathy* with others' experience, i.e. *compassion*.

The experience of getting in touch with the deepest level of our feelings and our most comprehensive, all-inclusive understanding of our own lives and the lives of others is clearly going to be different for each of us. But in general we might say that it is probably going to involve bringing to awareness our deeply felt longings, values and needs, and then remembering specific experiences that have allowed us to feel close to these longings and needs. 'Remembering', however, sounds a bit too much based in the mind or the intellect, and therefore doesn't adequately describe the practices of either reflection or meditation. Indeed, a memory can all too easily set off a chain of associations that leaves us, temporarily at least, without a focus. So to try to guard against this, we need also to use visualisations (of significant people, for example, representing different aspects of our experience) and, especially, to link our meditation process with a concentrated awareness of our breathing.

So, what sort of experiences can we bring to mind that might succeed in connecting us deeply with an underlying joy and tranquillity at the heart of our being? In my own case, I find myself remembering, for example, the delightful feeling of affection and of being 'fully in communication' that arises sometimes during a conversation with dearly loved friends or family members; or a favourite piece of music that suddenly arises from some mysterious place in my memory to express the state of my feelings at a particular moment; or the general sense of well-being that arises after an act of kindliness; or the sense of complete absorption when I am dancing or writing; or finally, remembering the deep but subtle shift in my feelings when an intense and longstanding physical pain suddenly subsides temporarily into no more than a sense of mild discomfort that seems manageable, almost friendly; and how this physical relief broadens out into a sense of general gratitude.

(You might find it helpful at this point to spend a few minutes listing the experiences that you personally find bring you into contact with this calm, positive foundation of our deepest self that we so often ignore.)

Recognise the Necessity of Compassion

The compassion aspect of the 'Mind Training' practice is generally seen by the commentators as its most important dimension and its defining vision and inspiration. Compassion is of course widespread historically and culturally as a key ideal for religions and ethical systems, and includes a number of different aspects and emphases. 'Empathy' (the ability to identify with others' emotions) is perhaps the central meaning, but other key terms are 'love', 'sympathy', 'care', 'pity' and (on an everyday level) 'kindliness'. But, as we shall see, the tradition based on the Atisha-Chekawa slogans gives 'compassion' an unexpected and radical emphasis, as in slogan 7:

Riding the breath, send to *others your own well-being, and* take in *the suffering of others* (Note 5).

The story is that the twelfth century Tibetan teacher Chekawa was inspired to begin elaborating Atisha's original work on the fifty-nine slogans when he became intrigued by the following lines he happened to see in a book while visiting a friend:

'Give all victory to others; take defeat for yourself.' (Note 6)

As a piece of ethical guidance this will at first seem for many of us a bit over the top. But its practical relevance as a metaphor becomes clear when we place it in the context of the many references in the commentaries to a familiar theme in Buddhist teachings, from the earliest texts onwards, in which the ethical ideal of compassion is symbolised as *maternal caring*. For example:

'Just as a mother would protect her only child at the risk of her own life, even so, let [us] cultivate a boundless heart towards all beings.' (Note 7)

Traditionally, then, the maternal expression of loving care typically includes an element of self-sacrifice, and this raises an issue that is, I think, nicely conveyed by a joke that I think I must have first heard in one of the radio broadcasts of the much loved Rabbi Lionel Blue:

"How many Jewish grandmothers does it take to change a light-bulb?"

Answer: "None. Don't worry about me; I'm quite happy sitting in the dark."

On the one hand, the joke presents an affectionate but slightly exasperated view of mothers' (and grandmothers') determination that their expressions of love and care must always involve looking after other people's interests and sensitivities rather than their own. There is underlying admiration and gratitude here, but the humour really depends on an implied criticism based on one of the central values of contemporary culture: the importance of 'standing up for your own interests', i.e. egotism. (Hence our surprise at reading the recommendation, 'Victory to others; defeat for ourselves'.)

The point here is that one of the main teachings in the whole Buddhist tradition is that all our various forms of egotism, both as a specific behaviour and a general principle, are the result of a complete *misunderstanding* of our experience, i.e. seeing ourselves as separate, individual beings (see Part One, Note 1). On the contrary, as we saw earlier, our individuality as separate beings is not an 'objective fact' but a mental and cultural construct that ignores our deep 'inter-connectedness' with others. Our symbolic 'Jewish grandmothers' are right, therefore: when we resolve to 'stand up for our own interests', to defend *our* interests *against* the interests of others, we are usually pursuing an unskilful strategy and perhaps even chasing an illusion. Indeed, many of the commentaries on the slogans begin by elaborating at length how each of us has only survived the vulnerability of infancy and childhood because of our mother's innumerable sacrifices, and recommend that we should base our whole ethical practice on fully experiencing our gratitude to our mothers and trying to emulate her example. So perhaps we should take the 'joke' quite seriously and say: *'Wherever possible, make sure that you are the one sitting in the dark!'*

However, there is an issue here that is much broader than children's occasional irritation with well-meaning mothers and grandmothers, namely the cultural basis for differentiated gender-roles. On the whole it has always been women who are brought up to feel that compassion – emphasis on caring for others ahead of oneself – is their speciality, their accomplishment, and their destiny. And indeed, modern societies are largely dominated by the typical male attitude that life is about looking after your own interests, competition, and the struggle for dominance. From this point of view, we can see the cultural and even political importance of the radical challenge posed for us by Atisha's version of the principle of compassion.

So, how should we *practise* compassion? What can we do to reverse our attitudes to 'victory', 'defeat', and 'standing up for our own interests'? Again, the breath is of prime importance: the wording of slogan 7 suggests, in a vivid image, that we should 'ride the breath' both in 'sending to' others our sense of well-being and 'taking in' the pain of others. We can begin our practice by simply *noticing* the current state of our mind and feelings – what we are most aware of in ourselves at this moment. This might be something quite physical and general (lack of energy, a familiar recurrent pain, or a sense of warmth and relaxation) or a response to a specific experience (irritation at a cancelled appointment, remorse at the memory of having made an overbearing or spiteful comment, or delight at the memory of someone's kindness). The effort of 'noticing' will almost certainly bring to the fore one particular element in our awareness, and we then need to breathe this down as deeply as we can into our hearts.

Whether we 'start with ourselves' (slogan 8) as senders (of well-being) or as takers-in (of pain) will depend on whether we initially notice the current state of our thoughts and feelings as being positive or negative. In either case, our general concern is always to develop compassion, i.e. using our imagination to understand and empathise with what is going on in other people's hearts and minds.

A sense of positive energy may have a number of starting points, including for example a feeling of physical well-being or enthusiasm for a forthcoming activity. Or we may find that we are connecting with a sense of *gratitude* – towards, for example, a parent or other close relative or a close friend – or any other person, for that matter. Feelings of gratitude may not spring to mind immediately, but generally it is quite a practical starting point for experiencing a sense of well-being, because deep down it is hard not to be aware of the positive contribution others have made to our lives in one way or another. Having brought a specific person to mind visually, we then breathe their image down into our heart, and allow their image to expand into a broader feeling of well-being and energy.

The next step is to collect up our positive energy, and send it out on the breath, perhaps accompanied by a sense of warmth or light, to someone whose current pain or suffering we are aware of, as an imagined gift. The qualities of our well-being and energy will vary, and we will need to determine which particular aspect of the energy we are feeling might be most helpful for the person we have brought to mind. Clearly, this will depend on our relationship with the person we have visualised. For a friend currently having a difficult time we might wish them tranquillity or confidence or, to an elderly parent, gratitude combined with an impulse of appreciation or perhaps forgiveness.

In the next stage of the meditation, we send out the positive qualities of our energy not just to a particular individual but to *anyone* who may spring to mind. Anyone, that is, who seems to need, and thus to call forth from us, our initial feelings of well-being, confidence, optimism, strength, etc. This might mean people from our family or our acquaintance or our neighbourhood; people we happened to notice as we recently walked through a shopping mall or people we have read about or seen on the TV news, etc. As we expand this sense of compassion more widely, we may find that our awareness of our own self (our own needs and hopes) is gradually superseded by a more spacious identification with the needs and hopes of other people's lives. In this way our compassion practice is a precise move against the egotism, the systematic self-orientation, that creates stress, destructiveness and anguish at the centre of our institutions and the personal relationships conditioned by them.

So much for 'sending-out' our positive energies for the benefit of others: what about 'taking-in' the experience of suffering? The first step here is to notice fully whatever negative experiences may be arising for ourselves. Perhaps we have just woken up with a vague sense of depression, or recalled an incident when we were treated unfairly, or remembered with remorse an incident from the past when we behaved badly, or perhaps we are just experiencing a longstanding physical pain with sudden intensity. Whatever feelings of physical pain or anger or sorrow surface for us, instead of trying to reject, deny, or minimise them we *breathe in* these feelings as a process of accepting them. Instead of reacting with worry, anxiety, anger, or self-condemnation – which may well make us feel worse – we recognise that these negative experiences will turn out to be – in the end – temporary. And we accept them as more or less familiar elements in the overall pattern of our lives that we are engaged in trying to understand. As such we are able to gather them, with the breath, into to a space within us where we can accommodate them. We can then allow this acknowledgement / acceptance of painful elements of our experience to transform the original pain into a renewed sense of well-being.

What then happens is that we bring to mind someone we are aware of as having problems or difficulties of some sort. We then breathe this other person's painful feelings into the mental and emotional space that we have made for our own pain, sorrow, anger, etc.

Although the wording of the slogans suggests that we send out well-being and take in suffering 'alternately' (slogan 8), this does not necessarily mean that the two are entirely separate. For example, 'sending out' our sense of well-being to a person we have thought of with gratitude may lead us to bring to mind elements of suffering in his or her life that we can also identify with and make part of our own consciousness, alongside our own pains and painful issues. In any case, although we may start from an awareness of specific individuals, the ultimate focus of the practice, as mentioned earlier, is on developing a sense of compassion that embraces quite literally *anyone* who in one way or another enters our consciousness – someone we love, someone we know well, someone whose face is familiar to us but who is nevertheless a stranger, or even someone we have merely heard or read about. So, like 'sending-out-well-being', the 'taking in suffering' phase also implies what we might call a potentially 'universal' dimension.

This leads to another important insight, namely that the pains and difficulties of our lives are potentially sources of strength. In other words, recalling the phrase that first inspired Chekawa, they can be just as much 'Victories' as 'Defeats'. Having realised that they cannot be dealt with effectively by attempting to deny or repress them, we come to appreciate that we cannot understand them except by welcoming them fully into our experience. And this means that our suffering is not just a personal problem but part of what Wordsworth calls 'the still sad music of humanity' (Note 8). But we need bear in mind that others' experience is never quite the same as our own, even though we share so much of our common humanity. The practice of compassion therefore always requires us, implicitly but nevertheless precisely, to use to the full our *imagination*. In the words of Shelley, written in 1821:

'Human beings to be greatly good, must *imagine intensely and comprehensively;* we must put ourselves in the place of another and of *many others*; the pains and pleasures of our

60

species must become our own. The great instrument of moral good is the imagination.' (Note 9)

Avoid the Poisons Arising from the Delusions of the Ego

Another slogan is always included in those comprising the 'Main Practice', namely:

'Remember three types of experience, three "poisons", and three modes of compassion.'

The phrasing of this slogan (usually number 9 in the traditional listing) makes it seem mysterious and elusive, but when we examine its underlying meaning we can see how it powerfully emphasises the practical importance of the Main Practice taken as a whole,

The slogan starts by simply offering a straightforward three-fold classification of our experiences, as positive or negative or neutral. Firstly, there are experiences that attract us because they strike us as pleasing or 'useful'. But there is a danger here that our responses may take the 'poisonous' form of *egotistical* desires or *cravings* that we are tempted to pursue without regard to others' needs. Secondly, there are experiences which immediately seem unpleasant or objectionable. The danger in this case is that our responses take the form of *hostility* i.e. negative judgements (equally egotistical in a way) including impulses of hatred, anger or contempt, which also 'poison' our thoughts and feelings. Thirdly, there are the experiences which stimulate in us a 'neutral' response, i.e. neither positive nor negative. This third response is in some ways just as problematic as either of the first two. Because if we think of a neutral response to experience as one of *indifference,* it might suggest a failure to understand the extent of our connectedness with the social and natural world of which we are a part, leading to a lack of proper *appreciation* of our experience, or in other words 'not caring'.

The phrases 'indifference' and 'not caring' sum up the nature of the challenge to which our attention is being drawn by this slogan, namely *egotism* – failure of sensitivity to the perspectives, needs and feelings of others. According to the whole Buddhist tradition egotism is *the* most fundamental of all human errors – involving both our understanding and our feelings. Egotistical cravings lead to a dramatic spectrum of irrationality (e.g. greed for money or material possessions, sexual exploitation, gambling, alcoholism, drug addiction), and egotistical hostility leads to another spectrum, equally dramatic: quarrels, conflict, crime, wars. The egotism of neutrality is a bit more subtle: a lack of concern or interest in our responses to nature, events and people suggests a failure of *appreciation.* This might be simply a lack of energy, but it may equally indicate that our self is in a state of being 'closed off', i.e. a lack of connectedness.

In contrast, the explicit challenge of the mind training teachings is to cultivate ways of connecting with others that are ethical, subtle and skilful. Firstly, we need to cultivate our capacity for compassion, not only towards those we know or to whom we feel a sense of gratitude, but towards *anyone.* So we would hope to be able, in the end, to 'love' other people without dependency or lust, and to appreciate others without possessiveness. Secondly, we need to respond to our adversaries in a way that *reduces* as much as possible our impulses of hostility, aversion and fear. And thirdly, we need to examine carefully our feelings towards strangers. That we do not know them cannot be an adequate ethical basis for indifference or lack of care, and to respond with indifference can be seen as, at the very least, a lack of understanding of our inherent connectedness with others, i.e. the poison of 'ignorance' (the commentators' usual term).

The key dimensions of this ignorance were explored in the earlier sections of Part Three. First: ignorance of the insubstantiality of any evidence we may think we may have to justify our judgements. Second: ignorance of the openness, clarity and sensitivity at the deepest level of our being, and thus ignorance of our fundamental capacity for connectedness with others. Third: ignorance of the principle of universal compassion underlying the teachings as a whole.

In the Buddhist tradition, ignorance, craving and hatred are the 'three poisons' that always threaten to distort our responses and our behaviour. And ignorance is usually seen as the originator of the other two, which is why increasing our *understanding* of the nature of our experience is the first section of the practice, and perhaps this is why the whole practice is usually described (albeit rather incompletely) as *Training the Mind.*

This concludes the description of 'The Main Practice'. Except that we must not forget the slogan that is always included in this initial group) which simply says:

Use the Slogans in everything you do!

Which neatly takes us into Part Four!

*****

Notes for Part Three

1) Richard Rorty: *Philosophy and the Mirror of Nature,* Princeton University Press, 1979.
2) Karl Popper: *Conjectures and Refutations,* Routledge, 1963.
3) The Vietnamese Buddhist Thich Nath Hanh has a beautiful word for this: 'interbeing'. – see Part One, note 6.
4) Ridgdzin Shikpo: *Openness, Clarity, Sensitivity,* The Longchen Foundation, 2000
5) The practice is called '*Tonglen*' in Tibetan.
6) Jamgon Kongtrul: *The Great Path of Awakening,* translated by Ken Mcleod, Boston: Shambala, 2005, Introduction by Ken McLeod, p.xiv
7) '*Metta Sutta*' in *The Sutta Nipata,* London: Routledge (Curzon Press), 1985, p.16

8) Wordsworth: 'Lines Composed a Few Miles above Tintern Abbey', 1798
9) Shelley: 'In Defence of Poetry', 1821. (Emphasis added and gender bias ('man'; 'he') removed.)

The First Ten Slogans

The Preliminaries

1) First, train in The Preliminaries

The Main Practice

2) Treat all experience like a dream.
3) Imagine the experience of an unborn child.
4) Remember that the emptiness of experience is itself an antidote.
5) Remember and enjoy the open, all-inclusive foundation of your being.
6) Treat your experience of the world as an illusion.
7) Riding the breath, *send to* others your own well-being, and *take in* the suffering of others.
8) Begin the alternating sequence of sending and taking with yourself.
9) Remember three types of experience, three 'poisons' and three modes of compassion.
10) Use the slogans in everything you do.

Part Four:
Slogans 11–59
Listed on Separate Pages with Explanatory Notes

(See page 72 for the index to the slogans)

Using the Slogans – Some Suggestions

It might be a good idea at first just to read through the slogans consecutively in order to gain a general overview of the sort of themes they contain. This would be a useful step as a sort of introductory familiarisation. But it is not what the slogans were intended for, and it is no substitute for using the slogans one at a time as part of a practical meditation repeated regularly, as described below.

Developing a way of using the slogans to guide your meditation is inevitably a personal process, and it is going to take a few trial attempts before you find a method that feels comfortable and helpful. But here are a few thoughts based on my own experience of using the slogans – some general ideas first and then some specific examples.

I always find it helpful to start by concentrating for at least five minutes on my breathing, noticing each breath as it arises, and following it in and out. When I find myself getting distracted I counteract this by *counting* the breaths from one to ten and then starting again.

When I feel I have more or less managed to let go of distractions (plans, worries, etc) by fully focusing on breathing, I then spend a few minutes reminding myself of the outline of the teachings, as follows (still accompanied by the breath, however):

The 'Four Reminders' are a good start – breathing them in one by one (See Part Two,). And then I remind myself of the different aspects of the 'Main Practice', usually in the following order. 1) Because our experiences are in an importance sense insubstantial, they are not *fixed* or determined. 2) At its deepest level our nature has a capacity for being positive, open, and kindly. 3) Our experiences can easily be poisoned by egotistical impulses. 4) The basic *shape* of compassion is that on the one hand we send out to others our sense of well-being and, on the other hand, we accept and breathe in our own and others' suffering.

I try to resist the temptation to fully articulate all this to myself in words, but to experience each aspect as a different sort of feeling.

The next step is that I try to become aware of my prevalent mood (sometimes arising from a specific event), which may be a combination of different emotional impulses – both positive and negative. Next I turn to the index of slogans and select one at random, noting the wording of the explanation, as well as the slogan itself. The mood and the slogan then together provide a focus for my mediation. This may lead me to visualise a specific person as a starting point for the sending / taking process, or perhaps it just creates a strong sense of the current state of my thoughts and feelings.

For example:

1) Noticing that my state of mind is rather 'low': I am a bit worried about physical symptoms and depressed by my reaction to them.

Random slogan 28: *'Don't hope for results'.*

Then a friend comes to mind who always seems rather depressed about his work, even though he works very hard at it.

Yes, this seems potentially relevant for both of us: my friend could perhaps focus more on enjoying the *process* of his work, and this seems to link with me *accepting* my injuries.

So now I sit and breathe with this awareness for ten minutes. And also, generalising out a bit: I find I am imagining a world where we *all* do things 'for their own sake'.

2) Feeling a general sense of comfort and well-being

Random slogan 13: *'Be grateful to everyone'.*
Suddenly and quite unexpectedly I feel grateful to a friend for whom I usually feel some irritation, remembering some pleasant but long-forgotten experiences. I imagine 'sending out' this experience to him on my breath, and imagine an affectionate conversation with him about those times.

The joy of this recurs several times during the day.

3) Feeling remorse about an interaction where I thought I had been insensitive, and yet inclined to blame the other person and feeling a rising sense of resentment;

Random slogan 32: *'Don't wait in ambush'.*

Yes, I had indeed started to elaborate my feeling of resentment and to 'wait in ambush', and resolved instead to 'let it go'. I then feel my resentment evaporate as I realise how my friend's anxieties might have been provoked by what I had said.

Now I breathe for ten minutes or so with a pleasurable sense of newly reinforced connectedness, both concerning this friend and also with things generally.

Page Index of Slogans

To use the page index, close your eyes and point your finger randomly at the page. Turn to the page number you have pointed at and use the slogan on that page as the basic guide for your meditation during the next day or two.

Slogan 11

In the Midst of Adversities,
Transform Adversity into Awakening

Notes:

'Adversities' can be both external and internal; i.e. on the one hand the distressing actions of other people and on the other hand our own inadequacies.

But our experience or awareness of such things can also be positive – an unexpected source of insight, and a starting-point for developing our understanding – of our own shortcomings, of possibilities for political action, and of the human situation in general.

Slogan 12

Drive all Blames into One

Notes:

Underlying all the various factors we may identify as the causes of a situation, there is always one thing which can rightly be 'blamed' for our failures to understand or act wisely. This is our general tendency to view matters *from the point of view of our own single, separate self.* This can take many forms – ranging from over-confidence, prejudice, greed, and self-interest to various subtle forms of self-importance.

Slogan 13

Be Grateful to Everyone

Notes:

And especially grateful to those who cause us problems; partly because they offer us an opportunity to put into practice our ideals of compassion and patience, but also because what we see as others' shortcomings may remind us of aspects of our own selves that we don't wish to acknowledge.

In aiming to practise gratitude to everyone, we also remind ourselves that in any situation there is an opportunity for us to learn. And we remind ourselves not to exaggerate our own individual achievements, but to remember instead what we owe to the contribution of countless other people.

Slogan 14

Avoid Confusion:
Remember the Fourfold Openness of Experience.

Notes:

1) Our experiences only *give the impression* of being real and substantial;
2) Our experiences only *give the impression* of being grounded in an external reality;
3) Our experiences are *not* grounded in the reality of external facts but in cultural norms, personal opinions, habits or even subjective illusions;
4) Our experiences are therefore *always open to many interpretations*. So that instead of insisting dogmatically on our opinions we can 'let them go', i.e. open ourselves to the possibility of changing them.

Slogan 15

Four Methods are at the very Centre

Notes:

1) Letting go of egotism through generosity and patience;
2) Confessing our remorse when we realise that our actions have been aggressive or self-destructive;
3) Remembering the central importance of compassion;
4) Having faith in our deep-seated positive energies.

Slogan 16

Anything Unexpected –
Include it in your Meditation

Notes:

'Anything': thoughts and feelings as well as events and situations; painful or pleasurable but especially those we experience as in some way *surprising*.

These are *gifts*: helpfully challenging us to reflect before we act, so that even our responses to the unexpected may be 'skilful' – free from egotism, and compassionate towards the sufferings of others.

Slogan 17

Five Types of Strength Include the Whole Practice

Notes:

1) Determination: examining our progress first thing in the morning and last thing at night;
2) Familiarisation: maintaining our awareness of the link between each moment of our own experience and the general principles of the teachings;
3) Integrity: arising from our meditation and the ethical quality of our actions;
4) Remorse: each time our practice falls short of its ideals, gently repeating to ourselves the key principles of the teaching;
5) Aspiration: reminding ourselves of our commitment to the well-being of others.

Slogan 18

Five Ways of Being Prepared for Death

Notes:

1) Determination: having confidence that we are fully prepared at all times.
2) Familiarisation: remembering that our experience of our death will be as insubstantial as all our other experiences.
3) Integrity: considering carefully how the manner of our death will impact on others;
4) Remorse: each time we forget that that our own life or death is no more important than the billions of other beings currently living or dying at this moment;
5) Aspiration: letting go of egotistical desires, and remembering instead the impermanence of all experience.

Slogan 19

All Teachings Agree at One Point

Notes:

The one point on which all teachings agree is the importance of eradicating *self-orientation* from our feelings and behaviour, i.e. the impulse to grasp, possess and judge; to seek what we find pleasant and to avoid what we find unpleasant; and self-importance – always instinctively placing ourselves at the centre of things. Only when we understand that our own ego is, like everyone else's, a cultural construct and thus insubstantial ('empty'), can we fully experience the equal significance of others.

Slogan 20

Of the Two Witnesses
Always Rely on the Principal One

Notes:

The 'two witnesses' – meaning: ourselves and other people. We ourselves are the principal, the most reliable witness of our state of mind and the state of our emotions. Other people's perspectives are useful but always secondary. Only we ourselves are completely familiar with all aspects of our experience, what we are really thinking and feeling, including our sneaky motives and hypocritical justifications. In the end, part of our strength is that we cannot deceive ourselves.

Slogan 21

Always Maintain a Joyful Mind

Notes:

Permanent 'Joy' may seem at first like a bit of a tall order. So it may feel more realistic to focus, more simply, on the sense of well-being and confidence arising from our awareness of having a clear ethical purpose. And so, even what initially seem to be a problem can turn out to be a help, Moreover, whether things are going well or badly, we should always remember to be kind to ourselves.

Slogan 22

Making Progress:
No longer Distracted by Distractions

Notes:

We don't necessarily fall over every time we stumble, and in a similar way one lapse of awareness need not distract us from our meditation practice. Indeed, noticing a momentary lapse can itself be the first step towards recovery.

There is risk that this line of thought can lead us into complacency. However, we do need to remember that feeling genuine remorse about our lapses of awareness may genuinely be a sign that we are making progress. The important thing is to preserve a gentle curiosity about *all* our experiences.

Slogan 23

Always Train in Three Basic Principles

Notes:

1) *Dedication to the benefit of others.* Avoiding the temptation of serving our own advantage (e.g. through subtle forms of self-aggrandisement and self-promotion) when we are supposed to be helping others.
2) *Avoiding display* – And any other form of ostentation, pretentiousness, or flamboyance, including display of how unselfishly we are behaving.
3) *Openness to **all** beings:* i.e. impartiality. Trying to avoid limiting our patience and compassion to particular types of people (i.e. those we like or who are similar to us), or only to human beings, excluding other forms of life.

Slogan 24

Change – But Remain Natural

Notes:

On the one hand we wish to change ourselves quite radically, by devoting our efforts to the well-being of others. But on the other hand we want our efforts to be inconspicuous and relaxed. We want to avoid self-important 'fanfares' and the conceit of emphasising our superiority, e.g. that it is always others who 'need our help' and never the other way round.

Slogan 25

Don't Talk about Others' Shortcomings

Notes:

Gossiping about others' weaknesses and failures can be a way of suggesting that we ourselves are free from deficiencies, and thereby boosting our own self-esteem. However, speaking critically about others behind their backs often doesn't feel good; and this can lead to a sense of guilt, so that in the end it can actually have the effect of *harming* our sense of well-being.

Slogan 26

Don't Dwell on Other People's Problems

Notes:

Dwelling on someone else's problems is often an indirect way of feeling superior, and this may arise from a feeling that our own merits are not sufficiently recognised. And anyway it is unlikely to be helpful. On the contrary, it would be much more helpful to spend our efforts analysing *our own* behaviour, because if there are problems we are more likely to be able to do something about them.

Slogan 27

Work with the Most Disturbing Problems First

Notes:

There may be some emotional issues where we are seriously 'stuck', creating problems or irrational attachments that disturb us deeply. (Issues concerning, for example, jealousy, guilt, anger, arrogance, sexual desire, complacency, etc.) And we may be trying to avoid these major obstacles by focusing our attention on the minor irritants in our lives (e.g. those that merely arouse our irritation or indignation).

But by focussing on these minor irritants we may be defensively 'holding on' to something which we would do well to 'let go', so that we can then face up directly to our more serious troubles.

Slogan 28

Don't Hope for Results

Notes:

To act in the expectation of some sort of obvious benefit is to set ourselves up for disappointment. Our actions and practices will not always or necessarily have the outcomes we hope for or expect; our acts of generosity may not lead either to appreciation or to generous behaviour in return.

Instead, let us think of what we do as undertaken for its own sake, accepting how things are for us in the present moment, and thinking of any beneficial outcomes as being a piece of good fortune.

Slogan 29

Beware of Poisonous Food

Notes:

Apparently tasty and delicious-looking food may nevertheless contain dangerous ingredients, and in the same way our meditation practice may be undermined by egotistical motives, e.g. thinking of it as an *individual* 'achievement'; enjoying a feeling of self-importance, of being 'right' where others are 'wrong'; wishing to be superior to others, or even wishing to be admired for no longer behaving egotistically.

So we always need to scrutinise our actions carefully – testing them for hidden traces of 'poison'.

Slogan 30

Don't be Predictable

Notes:

Our actions are predictable because our identity is expressed in established habits. But this consistency can be limiting. For example, we may always remember and return favours, but in the same way habitually hold a grudge for a long time in response to an insult or an injustice. This can mean we are *stuck* in our current habitual impulses, which can lead us to make *rigid* judgements. So let's be open to the possibility that on some occasions it might be helpful to be '*un*-predictable' – to do or say or think something *different*.

Slogan 31

Don't Speak Ill of Others

Notes:

Sensitively worded criticism can be beneficial, but it needs to be handled with care, because there is a dangerous pleasure to be had in criticising and disparaging others. It can be a way of showing off our own virtue, especially if we feel we ourselves are not being appreciated as much as we think we deserve. And anyway – we should always remember that our judgement of someone's faults may simply be wrong.

Slogan 32

Don't Wait in Ambush

Notes:

Suppose you have an objection to what someone has done – perhaps you consider that they made a mistake or perhaps you think they have wronged you in some way. Don't keep quiet and 'save it up', waiting for an opportunity to confront ('ambush') them with it later. Instead, either say what you have to say straight away in the most helpful way you can think of, or simply let it go.

Don't Undermine People
by Striking at their Weak Points

Notes:

No good comes of humiliating people and causing them pain by publicly drawing attention to their weak points. To do so is to misuse our power, or our position, or our abilities. And always bear in mind that it may arise out of our own pain, misery or isolation, and perhaps from our own seeking for appreciation.

Slogan 34

Don't Transfer the Ox's Burden to the Calf

Notes:

When something has gone wrong it can be tempting to shift the blame to someone else – for example, someone we don't particularly like, or someone who is weaker or in some way vulnerable. But the important thing is that we ourselves should shoulder the burdens that are our due responsibility.

Slogan 35

Don't Aim to be the Fastest

Notes:

As regards our spiritual and ethical actions, seeking individual prestige or recognition doesn't really work. In some things, being better than others is not the point. Much more important is genuinely wanting to do it well, trying one's best, recognising fully the support we have received from others, and being able to be happy for others when they do well.

Slogan 36

Don't Act with a Twist

Notes:

In some situations, the reasons for our actions will be complex, and the mind, under the influence of the ego, can be very tricky. So without our being aware of it we can sometimes find ourselves apparently acting generously but actually with a somewhat devious 'ulterior motive'.

So let's remember that 'being *straight* with ourselves' is important – and not always easy.

Slogan 37

Don't Turn an Ideal into a Demon

Notes:

The purpose of our meditation practice is above all a search for a genuinely uplifting ('ideal) state of being. So let's not allow our egotism to drag it down to something unworthy. For example, allowing ourselves, through conceit or complacency, to slip into feeling that because of our practice we are better or more deserving than other people.

If we do find that happening, let's make sure we treat it as a demon that we want at all costs to get rid of.

Slogan 38

Don't Hope to Profit from Others' Loss or Sorrow

Notes:

Sometimes we may find ourselves anticipating that someone else's misfortune may bring us some benefit: e.g. 'If she loses her job I might get the promotion.'

Or we may find ourselves responding to others' success with envy. It's as if we think we are all competing for the limited amount of happiness there is to go around. This is all totally mistaken, as well as embarrassing of course, and yet perhaps there's something comic about it. Let's try to eradicate it, but if we become aware of it, let's not despair, but notice it, then feel remorse, and then laugh at ourselves.

Slogan 39

All Actions should be done with One Intention

Notes:

Quite simply: *supporting* others: i.e. cultivating a benevolent state of mind; acting in such a way that what we do is of benefit to others and communicating in such a way that we try to create harmony and mutual understanding. Let us never be separated from this intention, no matter what activity we are engaged in: e.g. cooking, cleaning, studying, sitting and thinking – and even, so to speak (as the traditional texts say), if we are asleep!

Slogan 40

One Practice Remedies All Misfortunes

Notes:

We may be tempted to give up on our meditation practice because of illness, lethargy, or others' destructive criticism or because we are overwhelmed by our own negative states of mind: greed, hate, conceit, confusion, getting lost in useless speculations, or loss of confidence.

But at such times it is all the more important to keep going: summoning our patience as we sustain a sense of well-being in response to our difficulties, so that we can 'send it forth' to others in sympathy with their sufferings.

Slogan 41

Two Things to do: One at the Beginning,
One at the End

Notes:

Waking up in the morning: resolving that our actions during the day will embody our basic principles – generosity and compassion, remaining both open-minded and open-hearted. And before going to sleep at night, examining how far we have managed to live up to our aspirations.

However, even though a certain amount of remorse may come into play, let us be gentle – avoiding blame, whether of others or ourselves.

Slogan 42

Whichever of the Two Occurs, Be Patient

Notes:

When things are going well, let's not be tempted into pride, conceit or carelessness. And similarly, when things go badly let's not get down-hearted and lapse into gloom or despair. Rather than jumping in immediately with these habitual responses, let us instead respond with *patience*, continuing with our practice and allowing things to develop, one way or another, at their own speed, patiently allowing time for things to change, as change they certainly will.

Slogan 43

Practising These Two is as Precious as Life Itself

Notes:

We can think of our meditation practice as having two elements. At one level there are the individual mind-training slogans. And at another level there are the key principles underlying all the teachings.

Or we could think of all the moments of sensitivity and generosity that go to make up our everyday ethical actions, and, on the other hand, our general aspiration: to offer our experiences of well-being as a contribution the suffering of others.

The ability to sustain these two dimensions of our practice is what beyond all else gives life its value, its preciousness.

Slogan 44

Train in the Three Difficulties

Notes:

The first difficulty is recognising that some of our actions are destructive or unskilful, because the mind cunningly prevents us from seeing when our actions are really motivated by egotistical anger, ill-will, craving or self-importance.

The second difficulty is recognising that instead of such misguided actions we actually could do something dedicated to the well-being of others, rather than for our own benefit.

The third difficulty is sustaining our hope and determination, because when we do manage to change our behaviour we are likely to relapse quite quickly into our old habitual pattern.

Slogan 45

Cultivate the Three Key Resources

Notes:

First: Friendship: Important to make sure that we have a few wise friends to whom we are committed, who we wholeheartedly admire, who we trust, and from whom we know we can learn – because of their general insight, and because we know they are prepared to disagree with us;

Second: Commitment to putting into practice the mind-training teachings;

Third: A Moderate lifestyle: Remembering to be grateful that we are not hampered by the difficulties of extreme poverty, and making sure that we are not tempted or distracted by material luxury.

Slogan 46

Make Sure that Three Qualities Never Diminish

Notes:

1) Let us ensure that our appreciation of the paramount preciousness of friendship never begins to fade.
2) Let us ensure that we never experience any diminution in our delight in practising the teachings.
3) Let us ensure that at every moment, in thoughts, in words, and in actions, we try to put into practice our ethical values.

Slogan 47

Keep the Three Inseparable

Notes:

'The Three': Thought, Speech, Action. Or, more precisely: *reflective* thought, *sensitive* speech, and *helpful* action. They are inseparable in the sense that in order to succeed in establishing sincere, sensitive and helpful connection with others, we must ensure that at all times our meditation practice combines all three basic elements.

Without any one of them the other two are in vain.

Slogan 48

Practise without Bias or Preference

Notes:

Avoid responding according to whether you find something or someone attractive or unattractive. Let us try to gradually widen the circle of our compassion from friends and 'people like us' to strangers, the homeless, the disfigured, and in the end even 'enemies'. Let us interrupt our impulses to use judgemental labels and aim instead at *equanimity*.

It is important to allow this opening outwards to occur at its own pace. We can't force it or fake it.

Slogan 49

Always Meditate on What You Find Distressing

Note:

A disagreement with a close friend, for example, or with a partner, or with a parent, or perhaps someone has responded ungratefully to our efforts to help. Feeling upset is always a reminder to pay more careful attention, to *open* ourselves to this pain, or resentment, or bewilderment; and to *let go* of underlying assumptions and agendas.

In this way, by meditating, we can allow impulses of compassion, generosity, and patience to indicate a way forward.

Slogan 50

Don't be Influenced by External Circumstances

Notes:

It is tempting to feel that our meditation and our ethical progress *need* favourable circumstances, but we need to resist this thought. Favourable circumstances make things seem easy, and this can encourage us to become complacent. Instead we should see unfavourable circumstances as challenges that can stimulate us to develop, rather than as obstacles that we can use as excuses for allowing us to waver.

Slogan 51

Practise the Main Points Right Now, Without Delay

Notes:

This lifetime of ours is a precious gift.

What better way to take advantage of it than by meditating on the mind-training teachings; by developing our understanding through engaging with wise friends and learning from them; by seeking freedom; by benefitting others?

Let's not waste this opportunity! – Who knows if we will have another chance?

Slogan 52

Don't Get Things Wrong

Notes:

The teachings are complex, and we can easily get ourselves confused. For example, we can extend compassion and generosity to those who have no real need of either; we can be patient when we should be resolute; we can be helpful to people in various ways and yet not offer to share with them our understanding of the teachings; we can experience a greater sense of joy when we are publicly praised than when we know inside ourselves that we have behaved kindly.

So let us be clear and decisive in our practice, but always prepared to notice our mistakes and if necessary to change.

Slogan 53

Don't Switch Your Practice On and Off

Notes:

Putting a lot of effort into our practice for a few weeks and then not giving it very much attention runs the risk that the lack of continuity will undermine our confidence.

So let us be consistent. There's no reason not to be: we know that painful circumstances and favourable circumstance are equally helpful for developing our awareness. So we can aim at practising in a state of moderation and equanimity, rather than a state of extreme enthusiasm which we then find we can't sustain.

Slogan 54

Train with Your Whole Heart

Notes:

The teachings are elusive – so we need to allow them to permeate our whole being. Let us practice without hesitation or timidity or doubt, remembering how the teachings can help us increase the welfare of others as well as ourselves; helping us to remain single-minded and confident in spite of distractions, even if we don't always succeed.

Free Yourself through Examination and Analysis

Notes:

When our emotions have been enmeshed by difficult experiences, we need to examine the mind, seeing as clearly as possible which of all the many forms of egotism (delusion, greed, anger, conceit, jealousy, cynicism, laziness, etc,) are present. We can then analyse how we can liberate ourselves by means of the teachings; by sustaining our meditation practice, and especially by focusing on the welfare of others.

Slogan 56

Avoid Self-Pity

Notes:

Let us not get upset when things don't go our way, when we feel that our efforts and achievements are not fully recognised, or when others achieve more success than we think they deserve. It is always easy to give too much attention to the insatiable demands of our ego. Let us instead keep our hearts open, taking pleasure in others' well-being and trying to understand and appreciate the whole variety of our experience.

Slogan 57

Don't Be Over-Sensitive

Notes:

Let us try not to get irritated by others' behaviour or angry or jealous if we feel that their actions have received more praise than our own efforts, or that they have behaved badly towards us. Instead of an immediate, short-tempered reaction let us delay our response, try to practice patience, and remember occasions when we also have behaved badly.

Slogan 58

Don't Over-react

Notes:

Reacting with a strong expression of pleasure or displeasure to every little occurrence can be out of proportion, unnecessary, and wearing for our companions. Rather than reacting in this way with excessive and changeable emotions, let us aim to respond in a way that is careful, considered, and even-tempered.

Slogan 59

Don't Expect a Standing Ovation*

Notes:

Often, when people are not sufficiently eager in thanking us for our efforts, we realise that being appreciated was what we were really after! We know this is embarrassing, we know that we want our helpful actions to arise out of simple heartfelt generosity, and that explicit public recognition is strictly irrelevant.

But how hard it is: just to open our hearts and act generously.

Plenty to work on!

*Thanks to Kenchen Thranngu Rinpoche for this translation of the slogan.

Afterword

At first it may seem that meditation is basically a method of helping us to feel better about ourselves. And that is indeed a justifiable reason for giving ourselves permission to devote precious time to meditation, in the midst of all the pressures of busy lives.

But that is not always the main reason, and not the most important one.

Because through meditation we are also trying to develop a better understanding of our reactions, our impulses and our feelings, so that we can interact more sensitively and with greater awareness (and thus more *effectively*) with our family and our friends, with our colleagues, our managers and our customers, with our employees and our employers, and also, importantly, with our political opponents.

So that in the end meditation is also a way each of us can make a practical contribution to making the world we share with other people a better place – kinder, safer, more caring and more hospitable – for us all.

CPSIA information can be obtained
at www.ICGtesting.com
Printed in the USA
LVHW050333261120
672644LV00013B/693